THE SECRET OF THE BIG 5

Table of Contents

CHAPTER ONE: THE SECRET OF THE LION 2

CHAPTER TWO: THE SECRET OF THE LEOPARD 6

CHAPTER THREE: THE SECRET OF THE ELEPHANT 10

CHAPTER FOUR: THE SECRET OF THE RHINO 14

CHAPTER FIVE: THE SECRET OF THE BUFFALO 19

CHAPTER SIX: FINAL WORDS FROM THE BIG 5 23

GLOSSARY 29

CHAPTER ONE: THE SECRET OF THE LION

The Secret of the Lion.

The lion eats first before other's that is where we get the common saying "taking the Lion's share". The Lion's nature shows a pro-active habit for preservation by feeding itself first.

Lessons learned from the Lion:

1. Take money out for your saving before you start spending your income.

2. Develop a pro-active savings first habit.

Summary:

The secret of the Lion is by eating first ahead of the pack; the lion saves it strength and prepares for the future. It means committing to an automatic, fixed savings plan. This will help you change your spending pattern, so that even if you save small amounts, you will be developing a healthy savings habit.

Conclusion:

Once you are in the habit of 'eating first' like the Lion. You need to consider closely how to choose your own savings method. Several options are available to you; these includes,

1. Piggy Bank

2. Savings Club

3. A Savings Account at a Bank or Post Office

4. Fixed Deposits

For better understanding of the above you can meet a Financial Advisor or your parents.

CHAPTER TWO: THE SECRET OF THE LEOPARD

The Secret of the Leopard

The leopard's strength is a clear vision, a strong power of focus. He is totally goal oriented. The Leopard never aims for things it cannot get; it only and always aims for things it knows it can get. How does he do it?

The Leopards strategy is that it never lets its prey out of its sight, he patiently plans and moves towards its goals, never backing off, always staying focused.

Lessons learned from the Leopard

1. Have clear and specific goals that are realistic and inspiring.

2. Understand that it is important to think deeply about your goals, research about them, and the best way to get support for achieving them.

Summary:

You need to have a specific goal for your savings. You have to be realistic about your goals. Remember the Leopard always aims for things it knows it can get.

Conclusion:

Once you are in the habit of setting clear, realistic and achievable goals, and patiently planning and moving towards your goals. You are already on the path to becoming a great financial success.

CHAPTER THREE: THE SECRET OF THE ELEPHANT

The Secret of the Elephant

The secret of the Elephant is its knowledge, as the saying goes "knowledge is power" because of its prodigious memory, the Elephant is revered among animals of the wild, and it will always find its unerring way to the next water hole during migration. So other animals follow the Elephant herds during migration. The Elephant never forgets.

Lessons from the Elephant:

1. You need proper records keeping, to help you understand you're spending habits better. Knowledge is also power for financial planning.

2. Learn to do a budget at least once a year to know what you have or could get, you will know if you have any spare cash to increase your savings, or reduce your debt. Only a budget can give you that powerful knowledge.

Summary:

The strength of the Elephant is in its knowledge, "Knowledge is Power". You can build up knowledge of your financial strength by:

1. Learning what you earn

Understand what is coming in for you and how often it comes in for you.

2. Knowing what you owe

Create a careful record of your spending, so you will know exactly what is going out.

3. Draw out your future budget

Set out new targets/ goals to achieve and draw out limits for certain items create a control system.

4. Reviewing your budget

At the end of every month, compare your budgeted expenses to your actual expenses.

Conclusion:

Knowledge is power, only a budget can give you that powerful knowledge you need to achieve and maintain a healthy financial success. Be like the Elephant develop a financial memory, the Elephant never forgets but human memory is a little unreliable, hence only proper record keeping can help you acquire the power of knowledge.

CHAPTER FOUR: THE SECRET OF THE RHINO

The Secret of the Rhino

The Rhino's weapon is to charge when confronted by danger. When it is threatened, the Rhino works out what its biggest threats is and charges it down, taking swift control of the situation. Getting out of debt can be one of life's most difficult challenges, but it is also one of the most important things you can ever do. Learn from the Rhino by charging down your debt as fast as you can.

Lessons from the Rhino

1. Get out of debt quickly

Getting out of debt is a step by step process. Learn how to below:

Step 1. Face the problem; Know and research your debt.

Know the type of debt you have, what you owe, your repayment each month, when you will have repaid the full amount, which debt has the highest interest rate.

Step 2. Share your problem, develop a support system.

Think, who can support you while you charge down your debt? This will help you focus on goal of being debt free.

Step 3. Adjust your Budget, Revise your spending.

Revise your budget, so you can reduce your spending on just a few items each month. You then use the money you save to repay your debt faster. You will always find there are one or two places you can cut down a little.

Step 4. Create strategies to deal with your debt.

You have to work out which debt poses the biggest threat. This is often not the biggest debt you have, but the one with highest interest rate. You need to charge that one down the fastest!

Determine how you will deal with your creditors and their agents.

Step 5: No new debts, Stop yourself!

While you are charging down your debt, learn how to stop yourself from incurring any new debts. Also, stop yourself from buying anything on credit.

Summary:

Debt is threat, charge it down swiftly and take control of the situation. Identify the risk, pitfalls, limitations and unforeseen events that affect your budget, so you can plan and manage your debt and get rid of it as quickly as possible.

Conclusion:

Make sacrifices in the short term and charge down your debt.

CHAPTER FIVE: THE SECRET OF THE BUFFALO

The secret of the Buffalo

The mighty buffalo is deliberate and steady. It steadily grows its herds, diligently protects all the members of its family, knowing its strength and future are in its numbers. The Buffalo knows its wealth and strength is in its family. Even though building a large herd takes a great deal of patience, it pays off in the end. This is the secret traded by the financial institutions, they invest your money on your behalf to make it grow and give you back interest over a period of time, while your money remains intact and continue to grow.

Lessons from the Buffalo:

1. The secret of the Buffalo inspires you to grow your wealth patiently by investing it. Financial institutions will pay you a reward for investing your money with them.

2. it's important to leave your investment for a long period of time - so it can grow. Be patient and give it time, like the Buffalo it pays off in the end.

2. Choose investments that suit you and stick to them. To find investments that suits you, please speak to a financial advisor.

Summary:

Choose the investments that suit you, and stick to them. If you leave your investment for a long period of time, the investment not only grows each year, but grows exponentially. This means that you not only earn interest on your initial investment, but that interest gets added each year to the initial amount, and you earn interest on that interest as well.

Conclusion:

There is strength in numbers, be patient, be deliberate and steady, start an investment plan that suits you, give it time. It will pay off in the end.

CHAPTER SIX: FINAL WORDS FROM THE BIG 5

In putting it all together each animal of the big five has this to say.

From MR LION;

Make it automatic. As we have discussed, you need to make savings automatic. If you get used to the money not being in your account you won't miss it. So feed yourself first and take the savings amount out of your account straight away

And MR LEOPARD;

Great MR ELEPHANT says;

Determine how much you can save. The Secret of the Elephant teaches you to know what you earn, how much you spend and what you are saving, so that you can determine how much you can save. You might need to control or reduce your spending in order to save the required amount.

MR RHINO has this to say;

Monitor your progress. Take time out every month to review your savings and see if you are meeting your goals. If you aren't you will need to review your choices and maybe change your investment options. If you are meeting them or exceeding them then it will motivate you to continue.

And MR BUFFALO concludes;

GLOSSARY

Pro-active - acting in anticipation of future problems, needs, or changes

Realistic - having or showing a sensible and practical idea of what can be achieved or expected.

Strategies - a plan of action designed to achieve a long-term or overall aim.

Threatened - past tense or past participle of threaten, cause (someone or something) to be vulnerable or at risk; endanger.,

Investment - the action or process of investing money for profit.

Institution - a large company or other organization involved in financial trading

www.ingramcontent.com/pod-product-compliance
Lightning Source LLC
Chambersburg PA
CBHW030045230526
45472CB00005B/1689